D1542842

Farm Machines
at Work

Tractors
Go to Work

Jennifer Boothroyd

Lerner Publications ◆ Minneapolis

For Gavin

Lerner Publications Company
A division of Lerner Publishing Group, Inc.
241 First Avenue North
Minneapolis, MN 55401 USA

For reading levels and more information, look up this title at www.lernerbooks.com.

Main body text set in Billy Infant Semibold 17/23.
Typeface provided by SparkyType.

Library of Congress Cataloging-in-Publication Data

Names: Boothroyd, Jennifer, 1972- author.
Title: Tractors go to work / Jennifer Boothroyd.
Description: Minneapolis : Lerner Publications, 2018. | Series: Farm machines at work | Includes
    bibliographical references and index.
Identifiers: LCCN 2017053415 (print) | LCCN 2017055685 (ebook) | ISBN 9781541526105 (eb pdf) |
    ISBN 9781541526013 (lb : alk. paper) | ISBN 9781541527713 (pb : alk. paper)
Subjects: LCSH: Tractors—Juvenile literature.
Classification: LCC TL233.15 (ebook) | LCC TL233.15 .B66 2018 (print) | DDC 631.3/72—dc23

LC record available at https://lccn.loc.gov/2017053415

Manufactured in the United States of America
1-44569-35500-3/30/2018

TABLE OF CONTENTS

1 FARMS NEED TRACTORS

Tractors are powerful machines.
Farmers use them almost every day.

Tractors pull heavy
machines and grain carts.

Tractors save time and make
work easier for farmers.

Tractors come in all shapes and sizes.
Small tractors are easier to drive in
tight spaces. Big tractors have more
power to pull huge machines.

Tractor tires fit between the rows of crops in a field. Some tractors have tracks instead of tires.

Different tires and tracks help farmers drive across different types of soil.

Tractors have a hitch. The hitch connects other machines to the tractor. The hitch is very strong.

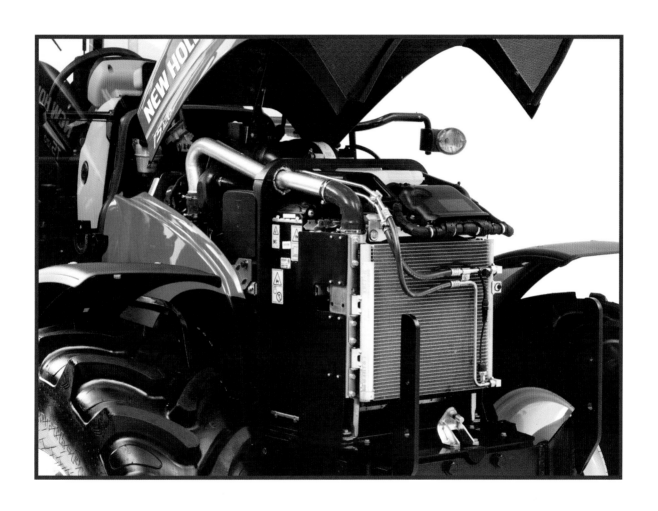

Tractors have mighty engines. The engine burns fuel to make power. This power makes the tractor run.

People sit inside the tractor's cab.

The driving controls are in the tractor's cab. Tractors have a steering wheel and a brake pedal.

There is also a control panel in the cab. The farmer uses it to control machines connected to the tractor.

Tractors work all year. At planting time, tractors pull plows and planters. Plows break up the soil. Planters put seeds into the ground.

During the growing season, tractors pull cultivators and sprayers. Cultivators stop weeds. Sprayers spread fertilizers to help the crops grow.

Cultivators also break up the soil so crops can get more water.

During harvesttime, tractors pull
grain carts and trailers. Harvesters
collect the crops from the field.
Trailers carry the crops from the field.

The attachment on this tractor is a front plow.

On snowy days, tractors push front plows to clear snow. Sometimes heavy chains are put on the tires for more traction.

TRACTORS YESTERDAY, TODAY, AND TOMORROW

Before tractors, farmers planted and harvested crops by hand. Later on, horses pulled simple farm machines.

Fordson tractors, created in 1917 by Henry Ford, were the first tractors to be built on an assembly line instead of by hand one at a time.

The first gas-powered tractor was invented in 1892. Early tractors had hard metal seats. Some would tip over if farmers didn't drive them carefully.

High-tech features such as self-steering let farmers focus on other work while the tractor runs itself.

Tractors today are faster, safer, and more comfortable. The cab protects the farmers from the loud engine noise or in an accident. Some have cushioned seats and even air-conditioning.

Future tractors will run on fuel made from chaff and manure. These renewable fuels will let farmers produce the fuel they need and will be good for the environment.

One day, this manure might power a tractor!

TRACTOR PARTS

steering wheel

controls

cab

tire

FUN TRACTOR FACTS

- Many tractor tires are huge. Some are more than 7 feet (2.1 m) tall.

- People compete in competitions called tractor pulls. Tractors pull heavy sleds behind them during tractor pulls. Whichever tractor pulls the sled the farthest wins!

- One of the world's largest tractors is 20 feet (6.1 m) wide, 27 feet (8.2 m) long, and 14 feet (4.3 m) tall. It weighs about 130,000 pounds (58,967 kg).

GLOSSARY

chaff: parts of a plant not eaten by people

crop: a plant grown to eat

fertilizer: a substance (such as manure or a chemical) put into soil to make it richer so that plants grow better

growing season: the time of year when plants grow well

manure: solid waste from animals used to make healthy soil

renewable fuel: fuel from sources that can never be used up

traction: an object's grip on another surface

trailer: a wagon or storage container pulled by a vehicle

FURTHER READING

My American Farm: CA Antique Tractors
http://www.myamericanfarm.org/videos/video_player.php?vurl=AH821_CA_Antique_Tractors.mp4

Nelson, Kristin L. *Farm Tractors on the Move.* Minneapolis: Lerner Publications, 2011.

On Track with Tractor Safety
https://www.progressiveag.org/uploads/documents/mystery/tractor.pdf

Roberts, Josephine. *Total Tractor!* New York: DK, 2015.

Waldendorf, Kurt. *Hooray for Farmers!* Minneapolis: Lerner Publications, 2017.

EXPLORE MORE

Learn even more about tractors! Scan the QR code to see photos and videos of tractors in action.

INDEX

PHOTO ACKNOWLEDGMENTS

The images in this book are used with the permission of New Holland except: Tatiana Kasyanova/Shutterstock.com, p. 1 (background); Brian A Jackson/Shutterstock.com, p. 6 (hay bales); Library of Congress (LC-USF33-006423-M3), p. 16; Topical Press Agency/Hulton Archive/Getty Images, p. 17; sheris9/Shutterstock.com, p. 19 (straw pile); Laura Westlulnd/Independent Picture Service, p. 23 (tractor). Design elements: enjoynz/DigitalVision Vectors/Getty Images; CHEMADAN/Shutterstock.com; pingebat/Shutterstock.com; LongQuattro/Shutterstock.com.

Cover: New Holland.